The Crimson Spider

Homer Lea

Adapted From *The Vermilion Pencil, A Romance of China*

Edited by Lawrence M. Kaplan

© 2017 Lawrence M. Kaplan

Editor's Introduction

Homer Lea (November 17, 1876 – November 1, 1912), was an American adventurer, author and geopolitical strategist. He is best known for his involvement with Chinese reform and revolutionary movements in the early twentieth century and for his writings about China and geopolitics.

He is best remembered as an adventurer for his associations with both the Chinese reform and revolutionary movements between 1900 and 1912, ending his career as Dr. Sun Yat-sen's closest foreign adviser during the 1911 Chinese Republican Revolution that overthrew the Manchu dynasty. He is also best remembered as an author and military strategist for two books he wrote on American and British imperial defense, respectively, *The Valor of Ignorance* (1909) and *The Day of the Saxon (1912)*.

Lea is less well known for his first major effort at writing a novel entitled, *The Vermilion Pencil, A Romance of China* (1908). He went to China (1900-1901) and used his experiences there to craft his novel. In it he depicted a colorful picture of Chinese rural life with a fast moving plot centering on the relationship and romance of a French missionary and the young wife of a Chinese viceroy. He originally entitled the novel, "The Ling Chee," in reference to the brutal Chinese practice of death by dismemberment, also known as the "death of a thousand cuts," but his publisher, the McClure Company, wanted a more acceptable title and changed it to *The Vermilion Pencil, A Romance of China*. Prior to the novel's publication, in the fall of 1907, he unsuccessfully collaborated with Oliver Morosco, the proprietor of California's Burbank Theater, to produce a dramatized version of it. He later completed an unproduced dramatized version of it in 1909 that he entitled "The Crimson Spider." In 1910, he collaborated with Richard C. Croxton, a U.S. Army officer, on a longer version of the unproduced drama, now renamed, "The Great Symbol." His story eventually became the subject of a popular 1922 film entitled, "The Vermilion Pencil," starred in and produced by Sessue Hayakawa, the Japanese actor and filmmaker.

The Vermilion Pencil, A Romance of China received widespread acclaim by many critics upon its publication in March 1908, including claims of being the first modern romantic novel written about China. The novel centered on the romance between a Roman Catholic Breton priest and the beautiful young wife of the despotic viceroy of Chekiang Province. The story unfolded in the city of Canton, Kwangtung Province, in Southern China, where the viceroy and his new wife, a tea farmer's daughter, lived. Being desirous of educating her, the viceroy asked the French bishop, who presided over the city's Roman Catholic mission, to furnish a tutor for her. The bishop, with ulterior motives of gaining influence over the viceroy, sent the priest to instruct his wife. Over time, the priest and wife fell in love and decided to run away together. Forsaking his vows, the disgraced priest and wife ran away and took refuge in the secret "Grotto of the

Sleepless Dragon," with plans to leave the country. Before their plans reached fruition, however, the betrayed viceroy, wishing to punish his wife with the brutal execution of "lingchee," made a bargain with the bishop to bring his wife back to be executed in exchange for a donation of valuable property to the Catholic Church upon her execution. The bishop then sent a delegation to retrieve the Breton priest and viceroy's wife back to Canton. While the priest was held under guard by Chinese soldiers, the viceroy's wife was moments away from her public execution when the viceroy suddenly died from a seizure. As her execution was about to be resumed at the urging of the bishop, the Breton priest suddenly came to her rescue at the surprise conclusion of the story. The priest's rescue of the wife was possible due to an encounter he had with a dying leader of a powerful secret society earlier in the story. At that time, he acquired a special necklace, a "great symbol" of the society, without knowing what it was. When, moments before the wife's execution, he revealed the "great symbol" to his guards, who were members of the secret society, they and other members of the society in the city quickly rallied around him to free the viceroy's wife.

When Lea adapted *The Vermilion Pencil* into *The Crimson Spider* drama, he added some additional characters, such as Amah, a servant, expanded some character development and provided more depth and context to parts of his original story. He selected the drama's title in reference to introducing a crimson spider into his narrative, which he never mentioned in *The Vermilion Pencil*. A crimson spider weaving a web to strangle and devour its victims symbolized his main characters becoming ensnared in a web of deceit and greed.

The following version of *The Crimson Spider* has been edited to simplify and standardize the drama's format, which was inconsistent, correct inconsistent and erroneous word usage and correct some misspelled words. The stage directions have been italicized in either brackets or parenthesis. Many words that were mistakenly capitalized have been lower-cased and words such as Yangching, a misspelled reference to the City of Canton, which was known as Yingching, have been corrected. There are exceptions, however, in reference to words such as "peculiarggems," which is not a proper word, and was most likely made up by Lea to be a synonym for peculiarities. This and a few other words have been left unchanged in the drama. The original drama is from the Copyright Office, Drama Deposits, Class D, Unpublished 1909, Registration No. D17497-17522, Shelf No. 20, 301, Reel No. 405, Manuscript Division, Library of Congress, 101 Independence Avenue, S.E., Washington, D.C. 20540.

Lawrence M. Kaplan, Ph.D., Editor
June 1, 2017

Cast of Characters

The Unknown

The Breton

The Viceroy

The Mandarin

Captain of the Guard

The Tea Farmer's Daughter (Afterwards wife of the Viceroy)

The Amah (Servant)

The Fortune Teller

The Cook

The Bishop

The Magistrate

The First Clerk

Priests, Mandarins, Soldiers, French Officers, Executioners, Etc.

Stage Setting for Prologue

[An early morning in the Spring.

Across the front of the stage is the old King's Highway, as it passes through the mountains of the Tien Mu Shan. In the foreground rises a hill covered with tea shrubs; on the right an ancient, gnarled cedar bent down over a boulder. The curtain shows a scene in the Province of Che-Kiang, a landscape of alternating valleys and hills where peaks, cascades and woodland intervene in fascinating confusion. Patches of orchards in blossom alternate with clumps of feathery bamboo fluttering on the edges of rice fields.

Here and there on jutting promontories thick with cypress and pine are pagodas, below these the dragon roofs of Temple buildings. Immediately beyond the foreground is a vale around which the rugged, broken mountains are clothed in woods of various sorts. Over all is the purple mist of early morning through which is shafted the first rays of the rising sun.]

Prologue

[*Enter Unknown and Breton with mountain staffs.*]

UNKNOWN: This is the pass, my son; the summit and end of your journey.

BRETON: I am not tired,

UNKNOWN: No. You are young and because of that your going down will be rapid.

BRETON: But beyond this is another summit.

UNKNOWN: Yes -- and beyond that a myriad more.

BRETON: Where sees this old road end?

UNKNOWN: It has no end.

BRETON: Where does it begin?

UNKNOWN: It has no beginning. Travelers come upon it by small paths and by small paths take their departure.

BRETON: Let us go on -- to the high mountain whose top is hid in mist.

UNKNOWN: I have told you, my son, that this is the end of your journey. Near by, a hidden, precipitous path leads down from the mutilated highway. You will find it, and -- go down alone.

BRETON: Alone?

UNKNOWN: Yes -- alone. (*Walks away*) You are to travel henceforth alone because your thoughts are -- up there. You are solitary because you are blind to the multitudinous wants and vices of man. You think yourself of God. You are not. You are but an instrument of the bishop; not to save the souls of men but to gain their possessions; these tea fields and orchards; these mountains and valleys, the dwelling places of this land. For two hundred years has our mission labored to one end; to gain possessions within the city wall of Ying Ching and you, poor utensil, must be bruised and battered in this struggle. Do you understand, you dweller in the alcoves of God?

BRETON: The tea pickers are coming down the mountain,

UNKNOWN: The tea pickers? Yes, yes. We have not waited long, my son.

BRETON: Have we come here to meet them?

UNKNOWN: Yes -- for eight and twenty years you have been hurrying to this place.

[*In the distance is heard the low roll of kettle drums and the shrill wailing of trumpets.*]

BRETON: Listen.

[*The sounds are repeated.*]

UNKNOWN: They are coming too, -- and -- on time.

BRETON: I hear laughter,

UNKNOWN: You hear what?

BRETON: Some one laughing.

[*Unknown walks back and forth, laughing grimly, mirthlessly.*]

> UNKNOWN: Laughter! You hear laughter on such a day as this?
>
> BRETON: Yes.

[*Unknown stops and moves the grass on the roadside with his a staff.*]

> UNKNOWN: Come here, my son. What is that?
>
> BRETON: It is dew on a blade of grass.
>
> UNKNOWN: What! Is that all? I thought it was a jewel. (*Strikes the grass*)
>
> BRETON: Listen!
>
> UNKNOWN: A drop of dew! You think you hear laughter! How we deceive ourselves!
>
> BRETON: It is not laughter.
>
> UNKNOWN: Is it music?
>
> BRETON: No! No! It must be the song of laughter or the laughter of song.

[*In the distance is again heard the roll of kettle drums, etc.*]

> UNKNOWN: How gaily man plays himself into his tomb! How upon this spring day all prospers toward decay! Do you hear that laughter song again?
>
> BRETON: No.
>
> UNKNOWN: You will.
>
> BRETON: (*Looking up the mountain side*) The tea pickers have come down from the upper terrace.... A young girl ----
>
> UNKNOWN: What! You see a young girl! Come here, my son... What is that?

BRETON: A crimson spider.

UNKNOWN: And that?

BRETON: The web.

UNKNOWN: And that?

BRETON: An insect struggling its way into the web.

UNKNOWN: Is that all you see?

BRETON: Yes.

UNKNOWN: (*Laughs grimly*) So! So! Only a crimson spider and its web. Only a paltry insect struggling toward its doom! Look again and read for what is writ ----

[*The roll of kettle drums and trumpets is now heard near at hand. Unknown seizes the Breton and forces him into a rooky crevice partially overhung by foliage. A sedan surrounded by soldiers, bearers, yamen-runners, etc. enters.*]

VICEROY: (*Leaving his sedan*) Is this the place?

MANDARIN: Yes, Your Excellency; it was here that my retinue was stopped by the song of the tea farmer's daughter,

VICEROY: Such things are unbelievable, Sir, the song of a tea farmer's daughter stopping the retinue of an emperor's mandarin! What tale is this you are telling me?

MANDARIN: I swear that it is true, Your Excellency.

VICEROY: This song -- tell me again, Sir, -- what was it?

MANDARIN: Your Excellency, I wish I could tell you of this girl's song and not steal from its sweetness by over-praise. It was showered down upon us from those tea shrubs on that upper terrace, intense as a mocking bird, yet vibrant with human passion. With supreme impulse, wild and clear it rose to the mountain tops. My retinue stopped. I got out of my sedan. It was past dawn; the sun's rays were just stealing through the purple mist. On every hand the murmur of cascades and the thousand choired chorus of birds seemed, in the stilled morning, but a part of the song that rose from the tea shrubs. So tempestuous was it, Your Excellency, that it made the hills ring with its echoes. It called, scorned, pleaded, threatened. Now bubbling, like the wood-warbler, with cadences of silvery notes; now rising as exuberant as the night lark to the very ear of heaven. It was triumphant, beseeching, full of defiance and mockery. Then with laughter, gently, softly as a child's kiss its echoes fell amongst those gorges and was gone.

  VICEROY: On that mountain terrace, you say?

  MANDARIN: Yes, Your Excellency, near where those pine trees ----

  VICEROY: Listen!

[*In the distance is heard the last faint echoes of a song.*]

  VICEROY: (*Summoning the captain of the guard*) Bring me that singing girl.

[*Exit captain and yamen runners.*]

  VICEROY: You have seen this tea farmer's daughter?

  MANDARIN: Yes, Your Excellency.

  VICEROY: What does she look like?

  MANDARIN: It is difficult to describe with words what the senses can scarcely comprehend, Your Excellency. Her eyes, I remember, are round and soft as those of oxen, while her cheeks, that I doubt not, are as softly textured as the almond blossom, the jealous sun has lacquered o'er with ruddy gold.

[*Enter Captain of the Guard.*]

  CAPTAIN: Your Excellency, this tea girl refuses to come. She derides you and calls us the wolves and tigers of your yamen.

  VICEROY: What! Refuses to come?

  CAPTAIN: Yes, Your Excellency; that is, unless she comes of her own free will and is accompanied by her tea pickers. Shall I bring, her by force?

VICEROY: So -- she derides me! My leniency toward the people thus provokes contempt for my authority; engendering disrespect toward ancient customs; and brings jests even upon the law's vermilion majesty.

MANDARIN: Perhaps, Your Excellency, the harsh and threatening actions of this captain and his runners inspired her with fear; and terror makes strange actors of us all. (*To the Captain*) Tell me the truth! Did you not fall upon her in the manner you lay hold of rogues; cracking your whips; rattling your chains and implements of torture until, with all the terrifying noises of your trade, you struck such terror to her heart that the very fear of you robbed her of all volition and so destroyed her discernment that like the timid deer she knew but flight though emperors waited for her?

CAPTAIN: Great Sir, that tea girl and fear have never men. She is as bold as innocence itself. She smiles when she should tremble and looks askance when she should moan upon her knees. She laughed authority into the dust; and said her song was for the birds and tea pickers; not for the wolves and tigers of His Excellency's yamen. She disdained him with her laughter; she mocked him with the mischief that capered in her eyes; she ----

VICEROY: She laughed at me?

CAPTAIN: She scorned Your Excellency in ten thousand ways.

VICEROY: Then let every male member of her family, even to the third degree, be bambooed. Let her parent be brought before me that such punishment ----

MANDARIN: Look!

[*The tea farmer's daughter enters surrounded by her tea pickers, and stands on the hillside.*]

Tableau Curtain

Act I
Stage Settings for Scenes I and II

[*An apartment in the palace of Tai Lin. This apartment is divided in two by a lacquered screen reaching from ceiling to floor of red and gold lacquer. Walls are hung with crimson tapestry and the floor is of alternate squares of rose colored and white marble. The apartment on the right hand side of the screen is some two feet higher than the one on the left. In the middle of the screen is a door and two steps that lead down. In the left hand apartment is an oval window through which can be seen the curved dragon eaves of the buildings, broad banana leaves and foliage of feathery bamboo. To the left of the left-hand apartment is a semi-oval doorway. This apartment is finished in Chinese style with teak wood furniture and jardinieres filled with flowering plants. The right-hand apartment is hung with a rose colored tapestry with filagree of gold. This apartment is furnished in Chinese style of woman's private apartment with ebony couches inlaid with mother of pearl mirrors, jardinieres, etc.]*

Curtain Rises
Scene I

[In the right-hand apartment meditatively opening and shutting a book is the tea farmer's daughter clothed in beautiful robes; moving about the room is a maid. Presently in outer apartment enters the Viceroy Tai Lin, clothed in his robes and moves restlessly back and forth looking impatiently toward the screen from time to time. The maid peers out the crevices and mutely calls the attention of her mistress, who scarcely deigns to raise her head and look toward the screen. Viceroy begins to work himself into a rage and claps his hands imperiously.]

Act I
Scene I

[The palace of Tai Lin; apartments of the Wife. To the right of the screen the Wife sits musingly in a chair with an open book on her knees, the leaves of which she turns meditatively. The Amah busies herself about the room.]

WIFE: It is a year, today, Amah, since that ---- that morning when the Viceroy, my husband, came upon our mountain.

AMAH: You grieve, my lady, and ---- and weep?

WIFE: No! No! No more. You remember, Amah, how long time ago I used to wash away the nights and days with my tears, then hope ---- then ---- then ---- Ah, Amah, think of the tiny folly of my little tears when all the five salt seas are made up of just such tears even before the time of Tao and Shun.

AMAH: The five seas? Are they tears?

WIFE: Yes, Amah; that is why they are salt; that is why men dread their petulance and why, when you stand upon their shores, you hear sobs, only sobs, Amah, for no one has ever known the sea to laugh . . . In it are myriads of monsters once the thoughts and pain that flow with tears and as such impregnate it with those horrid monsters that are born of our grief . . . . No, Amah, I do not weep . . . no more.

AMAH: Nor should you. A year ago you were but a tea farmer's daughter. Today ---- the wife of a viceroy ---- a queen.

WIFE: To be crowned, Amah, is to be unqueened. To sit on the foot-stool of kings is to feed on crumbs.

AMAH: Crumbs?

WIFE: But it is not that today ----

AMAH: No?

WIFE: I do not know ---- Listen! On that day when the viceroy's runners brought me down from the mountain-side, and I stood on the old road, I ---- I ----felt ---- Listen! . . . .

AMAH: (*Peering down into a large jardiniere*) That crimson spider is here again. Its web is half made and yet it weaves like mad. One would think it has a fly at hand, or perhaps . . . .

[*Viceroy enters outer apartment; looks eagerly about then clasps his hands. The Wife suddenly rouses herself; beckons to the Amah and causes her to listen to the beating of her heart.*]

WIFE: Do you hear? How fit struggles!

[*Viceroy again claps his hand's imperatively and the Amah hastens to him.*]

VICEROY: Is she coming?

AMAH: (*Bowing*) In a minute, Great Sir, just a ----

VICEROY: Out with you! I will not tolerate this! Not another ----

WIFE: (*Laughing softly enters from behind the screen*) Most impatient, Great Sir, you are angry?

VICEROY: No! No! The French priest that is, to be your tutor waits in the Hall of Guests . . . .

WIFE: Indeed! (*Turns away*) Then I shall receive him

VICEROY: (*Hastily*) Just a moment! Just a moment! (*She stops with her back to him*) I have a necklace of pearls . . . .

WIFE: (*Carelessly*) Yes?

VICEROY: You wish it?

WIFE: I have not seen it.

VICEROY: I am seated on the divan.

WIFE: I am standing by the screen.

VICEROY: Are you going to take these pearls?

WIFE: Are you going to bring them to me?

[*Thy Viceroy hesitates, gets up, then goes slowly over and gives her the pearls. She wraps them round her hand and wrist.*]

WIFE: (*Looking up at him*) They would be most beautiful did not the jeweled kindness that suggested them dim their brilliancy.

VICEROY: (*Bowing*) Yes, yes, pearls are a very worthy jewel ---- unfortunate women have not their attributes . . . .

WIFE: (*Haughtily*) What are they?

VICEROY: Why . . . . Time's incrustations

WIFE: (*With mocking chill*) Yes? Yes? (*Walks over to table where is an ink stone*) Yes, it is quite true that what Time adds yearly to the pearl it steals from a woman's cheek. But . . . . (*drops the pearls into the wet ink and stirs them round until they are a blackened mass*) you see they are alike in a way . . . . Isn't it strange? Isn't it strange?

[*The Viceroy stands immovable; The Wife moves over to him, rests her hands for a moment on his shoulders, than seizes his ears and pulls him down into a chair.*]

You are not angry? I know it was very wrong?

VICEROY: The pearls! The pearls!

WIFE: (*Scornfully*) Pearls! (Stamps her foot fretfully and throws the pearls on the floor) Pearls! From that pool of filth where the good of men is drowned!

VICEROY: (*Pathetically*) Would you throw all my wealth away?

WIFE: (*Laughing*) Does not a running stream irrigate more fields than a pond? Is there not more purity in a brook than in a stagnant pool? (*Pouting*) Why don't you be saving of punishments; be wasteful of mercy and treat greed as a rogue? (*Takes hold of his ears and tilts his head back.*)

VICEROY: Yes, yes, that is very true, very ----

WIFE: (*Letting go his ears and stamping her foot*) It is not!

VICEROY: Not true?

WIFE: It never happens.

VICEROY: That is so. (*I a relieved tone*) Yes that . . . .

WIFE: It is not!

VICEROY: What?

WIFE: (*Again takes hold of his ears looking down into his eyes serious, begging*) Will you promise me not to have any more prisoners beheaded this week?

VICEROY: Again?

WIFE: Promise!

VICEROY: Yes.

WIFE: And send away that thin, wicked lictor?

VICEROY: Eh? Yes, yes, he is a rogue.

WIFE: And you will build the hospital?

VICEROY: No! No! a waste of money . . . .

WIFE: (*Pulling his ears*) You won't? Not even for me? Not even for me? (*Her lips touch his ear.*) Only that one little promise, my husband.

VICEROY: (*Thickly*) Yes, yes.

[*He lifts his hands to clasp her to him but in an instant she is beyond his reach. Smiling, then laughing triumphantly and happily she leaves him alone and reenters the inner apartment. Viceroy walks back and forth in great agitation.*]

WIFE: Ah, Amah, once again have I filched a little mercy from the guarded purse of state. What a thief this prison has made of me! I plot and counter-plot to rob (*Exit Viceroy*) first the yamen runners of their prey; then my husband of his rigor and even the people a little of their tears and pain. Pilfer, pillage, plot and in this thievery find some happiness and in these stolen goods some sustenance.

[*Enter Breton*]

AMAH: (*Peering through the crevices*) He has come. The French priest is here!

[*Breton remains standing in the center of the outer apartment; the Wife peering through the crevices. Suddenly she bursts into a peal of laughter which brings a startled look of remembrance to the face of the priest.*]

WIFE: Priest, come -- sit here.

[*Breton sits down in a chair placed beside the screen. Again the laughter of the Wife.*]

Why, priest . . . your eyes are really blue! Who would have ever thought such a thing! . . . . Blue! . . . . Isn't that strange . . . . (*The Breton bows his head*) Look up! (*He raises his eyes to the crevices above his head*) Priest, if your eyes were not so soft, I would say that they were sapphires; were they not so strangely bright, I would say that they were as the sky when the moon loiters behind the mountain . . . . So these are the eyes of devils . . . . (*Laughs with unrestrained merriment*) Are you a priest?

BRETON:	Yes, a priest of God.

WIFE:	And what have you come to teach me?

BRETON:	As the Bishop has ordered.

WIFE:	Indeed! And what did he order?

BRETON:	To save your soul . . . . (*Wife's laughter interrupts*)

WIFE:	My soul ---- and he sent you to do this?

BRETON:	Yes.

WIFE:	How thoughtful of him! Why did he not send someone else?

BRETON:	I do not know.

WIFE:	You did not ask to come?

BRETON:	No.

WIFE:	Indeed! And if he asks you to go somewhere else tomorrow, would you go?

BRETON:	. . . . Yes.

WIFE: Oh, very well! I may not want you any more. My last teacher had the learning of seventy winters . . . . No, I do not think you will do . . . not at all . . . priest . . . . (*She drops a ring into his lap. He looks up and endeavors to speak*) Oh, you need not thank me! The ring is not for you. It is for your bishop who wishes to save my soul.

BRETON:	Yes, he wishes it.

WIFE:	And you?

BRETON:	I shall pray for you.

WIFE:	Indeed!

BRETON:	Yes, and I shall teach you.

WIFE: What?

BRETON: To love God and . . . .

WIFE: How monotonous you are, priest.

BRETON: (*Looking gravely up at the crevices*) No, to love God is not monotonous and to pray to him is happiness.

WIFE: (*Laughing with mock compassion*) I suppose you pray all the time?

BRETON: Yes . . . to Jesus the crucified . . . .

WIFE: Cruicifed! And what had he been doing?

BRETON: He died to save men.

WIFE: (*Sighing*) How useless!

BRETON: From the crucifix came the cross; from torture, salvation.

WIFE: How dreadful! What a people you are, priest; to worship such redemption and putting heaven in debt. Don't you know that only rogues or fools try to make themselves the creditors of heaven?

BRETON: I shall pray for you.

WIFE: (*Laughing scornfully*) Pray for me? When?

BRETON: By dawn and by night.

WIFE: Indeed. Pray now.

BRETON: You wish me?

WIFE: Yes.

BRETON: Eu, amantissime Jesu, qui sponsae sanguinum mihi esse voluisti ad pedes tuos prosternor, et meum in te amorem debitamque gratitudinem contester. Sed quid rependam tibi mi Jesu . . . .

WIFE: (*Amidst peals of laughter*) What a noise you are making! I never heard such sounds! You must not mind my laughter . . . . I cannot help it . . . . You never laugh?

BRETON: No.

WIFE: Has laughter no place in your heaven?

BRETON: God has never been known to laugh?

WIFE: Indeed! Then finish your prayer.

BRETON: (*Hesitatingly*) Mi Jesu, qui usque in finem dilexlisti me? Manibus es pedibus imo et cordi tuo inscripsisti . . . .

WIFE: (*Meditatively*) No . . . . I would not say that your hands are disagreeable to look at. My honorable husband told me that the hands of foreigners were speckled and covered with red hairs like the wood spider . . . just think of it! . . . . I should say that your hands are . . . . You can put on that ring if you wish. (*He does not touch the ring*) I said that you could put on that ring! No, no on the other hand; yes . . . now pray.

BRETON: O Jesu quam profuso mi . . . .

WIFE: You never smile?

BRETON: No.

WIFE: I suppose it all comes from this dull praying? . . . . Are you going to finish this prayer?

BRETON: You do not wish it.

WIFE: (*Petulantly*) I do!

BRETON: Ad sacram hanc aram ad hoc sanctum sanctorum, accidere ardens que amore cor . . . .

WIFE: Do you know, priest, that I was swayed, uncertain by a hundred petty fears at your coming? Yet your face is not annoying . . . no . . . no . . . not as those terrible English of whose frightful deeds and enflamed faces my honorable husband had been speaking. Thus we sin by proxy, priest, when least we know it, as on the other hand our unconscienced wants and hopes pilfer from the embossed casket of the future those pearls that crumble even as they are touched . . . . (*Breton looks to the crevices where she is speaking. She starts back from the screen in alarm.*) No. no, priest . . . you must not look at me that way. (*The Amah comes to her*) Do you think, Amah, . . . tell me, do you think that those are the eyes of . . . of . . . devils . . . .

Curtain

Act I
Scene II

[*One year has elapsed between Scenes I and II, Apartments of the Wife in the palace of the Viceroy. Time; before sunset; the Wife weeping bitterly.*]

    AMAH: (*Kneeling beside her*) Why are you crying . . . . Why are you crying?

    WIFE: Go away, Amah, go away! . . . . You cannot understand . . . . I do not know . . . . Go away . . . please go away! . . . .

    AMAH: I would lay my jade locket on the altar of Ma Chu or the Three Pure Ones if they would but clear the pented heavens of these tears. That French priest with his blue eyes has done this. Black eyes, being of honest folks illumine only as the lamp light and do not peer nor quiz into the shadowed corners of our lives. But blue eyes, those blue eyes the priest wears in his head, are the product of hell and with their fires they pierce these screens and our cloaked bosoms as easily as the sun streams through an open window . . . . And now that the evil is done and the curse has been laid upon you, my lady, he has gone . . . . With not a word he went his way as a thief gone out of a shop ---- as a hunter creeps away from his nets. He has gone, and these many weeks you have sobbed and sobbed and sobbed when you should have rejoiced . . . . It is ever thus . . . . It is ever thus . . . . On the loom where we are given to weave vice-regal robes, we web sackcloth or ---- perhaps a shroud . . . . (*Breton enters outer apartment*) Look! Look! He has come!

[*Wife peers through crevices.*]

    WIFE: (*Abruptly*) What, you here?

    BRETON: Yes, I have come back.

WIFE: You . . . you . . . .

BRETON: I have come back.

WIFE: Ah, Amah. (*Laughing scornfully*) He has come back, Amah. Did you hear? . . . . Where have you been?

BRETON: To the Bay of Tai Wan.

WIFE: Why did you go?

BRETON: I?

WIFE: (*Laughing unrestrainedly*) I? I? How poor excuses stumble . . . . Amah, bring me my fan.

BRETON: I buried a man by the Sea of Tai Wan . . . . Perhaps I should not speak of this?

WIFE: (*Indifferently*) Oh, it is immaterial.

BRETON: His was a sad and perhaps terrible should ---- He died and knew neither God nor even the image of the Christ, that I held before him. He dug his grave low down on the hillside where the melancholy chant of Eternity dirges its eonic plaint. Even until the last day shall they remain together ---- the living sorrow and the dead . . . .

WIFE: (*Sarcastically*) Amah, bring me my Jade scent bottle.

BRETON: (*Drawing from under his robe the chain and great seal of the Tien Tu Hia*) As I offered the crucifix to his lips he put this about my neck and swore me upon my own crucifix never to remove it. (*Wife laughs coldly and scornfully*) His last words were "Priest, this is the symbol of Invisible Empire; it shall find you life where you expect death and death at the appointed hour" . . . .

WIFE: (*Coldly*) Is that all? Amah, bring me my brush and tablet.

BRETON: No; within and about the hut, where he died, was a great company of armed men and when I rose from his side with this symbol upon my bosom they fell upon their knees and struck their heads thrice on the ground . . . . Three days ago I was set upon by bandits in the woods of Sun Dak. As they were about to slay me my robe was torn open and when the bandits saw this symbol they also fell upon their knees.

    WIFE: (*In terror*) They were going to kill you? Tell me . . . tell me . . . they have not harmed you?

    BRETON: It was this symbol of invisible empire that protected me even where the crucifix of my God availed me not.

    WIFE: (*Mockingly*) Give it to me, this Symbol of Invisible Empire. Perhaps I too may find life where now is only death; a little happiness in these endless hours of pain.

    BRETON: (*Starts to give it to her, then hesitates*) No, no, I cannot!

    WIFE: (*Coldly*) Oh, it is immaterial. Amah, bring me my pearl pendant.

    BRETON: You are grieved?

    WIFE: (*With bitter laughter*) I? . . . I?

[*She opens the wicket in the screen and coming slowly down sits on a stool with her back to him.*]

    BRETON: I am . . . .

    WIFE: (*Turning her head slightly toward him*) Yes?

    BRETON: I have thought about it.

    WIFE: Indeed!

    BRETON: Have I ----

    WIFE: (*Laughing mockingly*) Oh, yes, your, teaching has been quite delightful.

    BRETON: I was away a long time.

    WIFE: Yes?

    BRETON: I hastened back.

WIFE: On account of my studies, I suppose?

BRETON: (*Hesitatingly*) Yes.

WIFE: How thoughtful of you!

BRETON: I enjoy----

WIFE: You do? Don't you suppose I know that? Instruct! Instruct! Instruct! I am tired of it!

BRETON: You do not wish ----

WIFE: No, I don't! What is the good of all this learning; all these black books? Who loves me any more for it? Does it add a dearer pink to my cheek? Do you think it gives luster to my eye or music to my words? Do you think it will puff away wrinkles? A cosmetic ---- a tire ---- woman ---- a ---- a ---- (*Stamping her foot*) I tell you, priest, I will have no more of it ---- never!

BRETON: Learning enlightens ---- it is a mirror ----

WIFE: (*Laughing bitterly*) Oyah! A mirror! So is a tub of water holding the image of the sun, but what warmth comes from that reflection? I would like you to tell me, priest, with all your learning, what there is substantial in a reflected image? What if learning were the painting of the world's ocean acts, could fish dwell in its mock waters? And I would like to know if there is the fragrance of one rose in ten myriad miles of embroidered flowers? . . . .

BRETON: Did you study?

WIFE: Oh, yes. I learned many things. In the first place that learning is like dragging the sea for the jewels of night. I also learned that the fairest sunrise fades the soonest and that a brilliant cloud is easily scattered; that trees blown away by passing winds have more branches than . . . . (*The tapping of her foot ---- she speaks as if to herself, her voice full of bitterness*) But why should I grieve? No one cares for me; no one ever thinks of me caged here, forever in this cold, gilded chamber, while they move far and wide, gay travelers on the many rivers of life. Now and then one stops and with a small laugh drops a crumb between my bars and passes on. They loiter through the world's flower gardens and I ---- I ---- sometimes there comes swiftly past a whiff of perfume. They drain deep the different wines of pleasure, while into my tiny cup, bar fastened, is poured a few drops of water. They move abroad under the wide sunlight, and

I ---- moveless in this wee shadow. They hear that great symphony, the world's, laugh, and I ---- no one ever laughs alone. Their cheeks are stained by the dews of a hundred skies, mine ---- by tears. They sleep that they may hasten the morrow, and I ---- to forget today. They weave and I untangle. Their threads are of a hundred hues, mine ---- one sad color. Untangling! Untangling! And when will it all end? Today is yesterday; yesterday as days gone: tomorrow ---- oh, if I only did not know! If I only did ---- (*Bursts into tears*)

BRETON: Your husband loves you . . . . Your husband . . . .

WIFE: What do you know about love?

BRETON: It is something from God . . . .

WIFE: (*Mocking*) Yes! Indeed! Why I thought it was just a violet thrown in a rocky waste; a sunbeam cast upon a cold sea, dew dropped into the desert; a bundle of burnt prayers tossed upon the wind ---- a ---- a ---- (*Tears*)

BRETON: Don't ---- don't ----

WIFE: You . . . don't . . . care.

BRETON: No . . . no . . . .

WIFE: I know you don't . . . . How I wish I were dead!

BRETON: No! Do not say that!

WIFE: (*Fiercely*) And why shouldn't I? One is better dead than one's heart strangled by this silken scarf. Why must one live forever on this desert, scanning the sky-line each day for what cannot come?

BRETON: You have been unhappy?

WIFE: Unhappy? Did you say unhappy? (*Laughing bitterly*) Why ---- I have laughed and sung each hour of the day away; no bird in all the park has been gayer than I, and my cheeks? Oh, I whitened them; they became so ruddy. How happy . . . how happy . . . . (*Mocking laughter. Turning to the Breton*) Don't you know ---- don't you know that I have not laughed nor sung all these weeks? No caged bird ever ---- ever---- I think you would have cared if you could have seen me cowering now in one corner, now in another; counting the moments for the coming of day; then longing for night. And, oh, how ill I have been; now burning with fever, then cold, chilling. I did not know what had happened to you; one little thought parched my lips, making my heart shrink and draw high into my throat. A noise like a foot-fall would make it beat so painfully I could not breathe, and when I heard someone coming, I trembled all over. I grew feverish, then cold ---- a dimness would come over my eyes. All day and night I cried for tardy sleep ---- and when one begs for sleep is it not a wish for death? (*Striking the palms of her hands together*) Oh, if you only knew . . . . (*Rising from her stool and looking at him*) If you only knew . . . . (*Breton stands as she comes close to him with her hands clasped on her bosom*) Tell me you will not go away again (*Their robes touch*) Tell me (*She rests her hands on his shoulders*) Promise me! (*She slowly raises her arms and puts them around his neck. Her face is suffused with happiness*) You will promise me . . . . Yes, yes . . . . Why did you not tell me that you loved me?

[*The Breton struggles. Presently takes hold of her wrists, unclasps her arms and puts her away from him. She falls to the floor as he passes from the apartment.*]

Curtain

Act II
Stage Setting for Scene I

[*A Street scene in China.*

The fronts of the houses whimsically carved according to Chinese architecture emblazoned with signs of lacquer and gold and with windows oval, square and oblong. Crowds are passing back and forth; Taoist monks beating their cymbals, merchants in their silken robes, soldiers in red jackets, peddlers with baskets slung across shoulders, etc.

As darkness settles over the city, tasseled, silken, emblazoned lanterns begin to glimmer from every projection; from balconies and carved fantastic eaves.]

Act II
Scene I

[*A street scene in the city of Yangching at dusk. The Breton, haggard with head bowed on his bosom passes across the stage. Natives of the city precede and follow him. An itinerant cook and fortune teller (F.T.) are packing up their wares.*]

F.T.: (*In the Cook's ear*) Again!

COOK: Again? Again? What again? Rice....

F.T: Did I not prognosticate?

COOK: Pork....

F.T.: Look! Again he is there!

COOK: So he is! So he is!

F.T.: Did I not foretell it; Master Cook, did I not prognosticate?

COOK: (*Doubtfully*) Yes, ... that is a fact....

F.T.: Cook, I see everything, hear everything, know everything. Now, Master Cook, let me do you a good turn; it will only cost you....

COOK: But he his been there for nearly two full moons.

F.T: Certainly! Certainly! But would he have been there if it had not been for my prognostications?

COOK: That may be; that may be.

F.T: Master Cook, let me prognosticate you. It will only cost....

COOK: No! But I do not like that influence just at my night cooking.

F.T: It is very bad! I would not be you for all the cash in the city.

COOK: What is it? Tell me, Master, tell me.

F.T: (*Jumping back dramatically*) I am overwhelmed, speechless, a dying phoenix.... Master Cook, you pretend to be a merchant and yet you are unable to distinguish great profits from a fly's head. Is it not known among honorable merchants that just scales and full measure injure no man? I am pained.... Good-bye, Master Cook.... Master Cook I leave you with pitying heart. Farewell.

COOK: What have I done? What have I done?

F.T: What have you done? What have you done but throw out the refuse, the burnt scraps, the very swill of your inquisitiveness to lure from me the peculiarggems of my knowledge . . . my pearly prognostications!

COOK: But what have I done?

F.T: Can you get rice without planting? Chickens without eggs? Heat without fuel? Prognostications without incentives?

COOK: But what threatens me?

F.T: Master Cook I should be lenient with you; that you do not understand the incomprehensible is not your fault. Cook, I pity you; to me only is apparent the disaster overpending. I will aid you.

COOK: Do Master, do!

F.T: Before prognosticating, Cook, I must have four rice cakes cooked well in oil and two pieces of pork.

COOK: Too much, Master Fortune Teller, too much!

F.T: Cook, I salute you! Tonight, empty your oil into the street; scatter your flour upon the night winds . . . you will need them no more. Farewell; there comes a day when every tumor must toe punctured. Listen now to my last prognostication; do not waste your wife's cash in mock money. It will not avail you! (*Moves slowly away*)

COOK: Master Fortune Teller! Master Fortune Teller!

F.T.: What is it, unfortunate man?

COOK: I will give you one rice cake and one piece of fat pork.

F.T: Does one grain of planted rice produce as much as four?

COOK: I am a poor man.

P.T.: Must not the poor avert their fate as well as the rich.

COOK: I will give you two rice cakes and a piece of lean pork.

F.T: You are indeed a poor man and unfortunate. Yes, my compassion pleads for you. I will prognosticate. Yes, two cakes, two fat pieces of pork and a bowl of kale.

COOK: Too much! Too much! I will give you the cakes and the pork. No more! No more!

F.T: Let it be . . . But mark you, Master Cook, the depth of my benevolence! (*Finishes his repast*) What do you see, Cook?

COOK: (*Whispers*) He is still there.

F.T: What else do you see?

COOK: He stares like a big-eyed owl.

F.T: What is an owl?

COOK: A bird of evil omen.

F.T.: What else do you know?

COOK: That he never turns his eyes away from the gates of Tai Lin.

P.T: What is a gateway?

COOK: It is the coming in and going out.

F.T: It is the portal of the dead and he would hold converse with something that is dead.

COOK: (*Hoarsely*) Is it that, master, is it that?

F.T: Did you not see him many moons ago when he used to go through that gate to teach ---- who knows what ---- to the beautiful wife of the Viceroy?

COOK: Yes, master, yes. He was as stalwart as a young bullock. He was a lion of India in those days.

F.T: And now he is like a specter, a troubled ghost whose Feng Shui has been ruined.

COOK: It is true, master, it is true ... He is as meager as pain itself.

F.T: (*Tragically*) Have you not noticed that since he came you have drowsed much and been careless of your business?

COOK: Yes. Yes. Two whole cakes and two pieces of fat pork. There is no end to my madness, no end!

F.T: Have you not noticed that when his fingers twitch men shun you?

COOK: Many men have passed me by, master, many man have passed me by!

F.T: Have you not noticed that when his bosom heaves out you have a sadness in your chest?

COOK: Yes, yes, right in here!

F.T: He has the appearance of a foreigner.

COOK: (*In great alarm*) What!

F.T: He is a foreign devil! Have you seen his eyes? They are blue!

COOK: Blue! Master, blue!

F.T: If he should look into your boiling oil, it would go up in flame; if he should look into your flour it would frisk with weevils; if he should look into your meat, lo! there would be nothing but maggots! And if he should peer into your heart ... tremble! (*Cook crouches closer*) Cook, how is the Idol of Yang Sau made?

COOK: By three swings of the axe, master.

F.T.: How is the idol of Yen Wang made?

COOK: I do not know! I do not know!

F.T: It is carved by tears, Cook, as rocks are cut by mountain rains. Its visage is of the terriblest sorrow; the height of heaven, the depth of sea cannot encompass it! Cook, he has the face of Yen Wang the God of Death!

COOK: I feel that sadness! I feel that sadness!

F.T: Cook, there are some things that are known and some things that are not. From the things that are known, we learn concerning the things that are not; but this is the task of the wise. Now, it is known that heaven is round and the earth square . . . .

COOK: (*In great excitement*) I see fire coming out of his eyes . . . .

F.T: Cook, do not hinder me! It is known, I tell you, that the heavens are round and the earth square; that the stars are shining characters in the Book of Fate, and eclipses are Dragon Feasts . . . .

COOK: There is a Dragon of the White God under his robe . . . .

F.T: Cook, be dumb! Such observations are reserved for scholars. Now listen! When tigers plunge into the sea, they become sharks and sparrows falling into the water are changed into oysters; dragons; . . . .

COOK: (*Huskily*) The Dragon of the White God under his robe . . . .

F.T: You think it is a dragon. You are a fool . . . . (*Mysteriously*) Cook, do you know what is said in the underground passages? It is said that the Deluge is going to rise; that a blue-eyed priest of the Western God wears the Great Symbol under his robe. Men of the brotherhood have seen it . . . . Hush! That is what struggles! When he wears this on his bosom uncovered, the sun will shine out red in the east; the five flags will rise of their own accord from secret places; then ten million men will come forth out of cellars and palaces; ten million thumbs will point to heaven and the dynasty will be destroyed in flames. . . .

COOK: Look! Look! The fire comes out of his eyes!

F.T: Cook, those fires are tears, but not such as you know. When you weep your tears are water; welling up from sorrow, they are bitter; being bitter, they are salt. In this priest something more than sorrow has laid hold of him; the watery element has been consumed and he now ejects flames . . . .

COOK: Let me go, Master Fortune Teller, let me go!

F.T: (*Laying hold of the Cook and whispering fiercely*) When that Symbol shines, it is the eye of a nation's wrath. When you hear Hung Shun Tien it is the growl of the Five Gods. When the thumbs of men point upward, it is our secret sign with heaven. If you do not follow the Symbol, thunder will annihilate you.

>   COOK: (*Struggling*) I will not stay, Master Fortune Teller, I will not stay!

>   F.T: (*Holding him fast*) Cook, you shall follow on that appointed day for all shall wear the sign of Shou; scholars, laborers, merchants, mechanics, Confucianists Buddhists, Taoists, thieves, officials, pirates, all, all shall follow. If you show duplicity, you shall die beneath ten thousand knives.

>   COOK: (*In intense excitement*) Look! Look! Something else moves under his robe! See!

>   F.T: Hush, Cook. That is the crimson spider under the Symbol of the Deluge. It is spinning. In and out his heart it goes . . . weaving, weaving and in its webs hopes, like little flies, and caught and strangled and devoured. When this crimson spider falls upon you, Cook . . . .

>   COOK: He is coming! He is coming!

[*Exit Cook and Fortune Teller stumbling and pulling one another. Enter Breton.*]

Curtain

Act II
Scene II

[*The Viceroy's palace; apartments of the Wife. Night. The indistinct light of the rising moon sends in a faint glimmer through the window of the court. The moon continues to rise until at the end of the act it is shining full into the room. The curtain rises on the Wife alone in the outer apartment sitting on her stool beside the Breton's chair; weeping softly. Enter Breton.*]

>   BRETON: I have come back.

>   WIFE: You?

>   BRETON: Yes, I have come back to you,

WIFE: Why?

BRETON: I understand it all now.

WIFE: You understand?

BRETON: Yes, yes, in these last few months it has all come to me . . . . You remember when your hand touched my robe? At first I thought it was the hand of God, for it seemed as though I were in heaven. Then came another thought and I cast you aside . . . . That was many months ago. For this I have suffered . . . . In every soft sound of the night I have heard you fall again and again, without a cry ---- Just a silken crash. In the day I stood before the portal of your gate. During the night I prayed, did penance, and sleeplessly watched for the reluctant shadows of dawn, a dawn that punished me with its thousand memories; with the larks' song fluttering from their bamboo cages; with flowers whose fragrance choked and whose colors burned my eyes; with laughter and . . . and . . . that dreadful crinkling of silk when . . . when I put you away, . . . when I threw you to the floor . . . . Again in the night I always stood upon the bank of the river for it was kind to me, with the tones of your voice . . . even the stars stole their lights from your eyes and in reproachful pain looked down upon me.

WIFE: And you have come back because of this?

BRETON: Yes, yes, and because of these. (*Takes some papers from his bosom*) Three days ago I found them laid secretly beside my crucifix. The Unknown put them there and now he is gone . . . . (*Handing her a paper*) Do you know what that means? It is a crimson spider. (*Handing her another paper*) That is a dragon; do you know its meaning? And this is the Symbol I wear about my neck. That is his letter and in that letter the Unknown asked me to go away for, it was a sin to remain. Of this I took counsel of God and for two nights I prayed to our Christ on his crucifix. Today at dawn, God bade me go . . . .

WIFE: Did your God tell you to come here?

BRETON: Yes, he told me to come back to you.

WIFE: To me!

BRETON: Yes, you have no husband, for husbands are searched out by God as wives are sent by him from heaven. On the second night before my crucifix all things became clear to me and doubts were brushed aside.

WIFE: I have no husband? I have no husband?

BRETON: No. You have no husband.... we will go away together to another country... to America where all are free; to Australia where all are forgotten or to another land where men are lost. We will always be together. I can look at you and you can put your hand on my shoulder... and it will be as in heaven.... We will live together forever, for whom God marries he never parts.

WIFE: He never parts?

BRETON: No! No! I have planned how we shall leave the city.

WIFE: We shall go away... together?

BRETON: Yes. You know no one can leave the city by night, but on the eve of the Propitiation of the Gods of the Waters, all the city gates will be open. You can leave the park by the western postern and I will meet you there the second hour after darkness.

WIFE: You wish me to go away?

BRETON: Yes.

WIFE: You wish me to go away and leave my husband?

BRETON: Yes, we will go away from China.

WIFE: No, no, I cannot, I must not go!

BRETON: I have thought carefully of all this and have planned that when you come to the postern gate, I will meet you with a sedan chair. I will take you to the river where there will be a boat waiting. Then we will go up the river to the Grotto of the Sleepless Dragon. Men fear this cavern but there is no danger. We can stay there until people forget.

WIFE: Until people forget! Until people forget!

BRETON: Yes, until all forget.

WIFE: And you?... and you?

BRETON: Will you go?

[*Wife goes over to window and remains for some time then returns and stands beside the Breton.*]

    WIFE: I will go.

[*Breton kneels at her feet, leans forward until his head touches her robe.*]

    I knew you would come back. When I touched your robe and felt you tremble I knew that you loved me and when you took hold of my wrists you do not know what happiness came over me. I felt as if you were going to pick me up and fly away forever to that heaven you have spoken of so often. The . . . then, you threw me to the floor.

    BRETON: You are going away with me?

    WIFE: You must not look that way. Don't you know that that was a happier parting than the first time you went away; when you left me without a word ---- chained by torturing doubts. But this time you threw me to the floor and then I knew that you loved me. I have not been unhappy, nor have I been joyful these many weeks, but I have been content and in the airy tapestry of my dreams I have embroidered ten thousand times just such a scene as this. Each day at that time, when you were accustomed to come, I sought my stool here beside the screen and waited and waited. Weeks and months have I waited. Now you have come as I knew you would.

    BRETON: You are going away with me, away from China?

    WIFE: (*Laughing softly*) Yes, I am going away to your Gods and heavens.

Curtain

Act III
Scene I

Stage Setting for Act III, Scene I

[*Bishop's study in the Catholic Mission of Yang Ching. A somber room surrounded with elements of religious meditation and devotion. Bishop pallid and thoughtful sits at table cracking his fingers.*]

Act III
Scene I

[*In the study of the Bishop of Yangching. Bishop seated by table. Enter a priest.*]

BISHOP: Well, what news?

1st PRIEST: The hiding place of the fugitives has been found.

BISHOP: Where?

1st PRIEST: They are hid in the Grotto of the Sleepless Dragon.

BISHOP: The Grotto of the Sleepless Dragon?

1st PRIEST: Yes, it is a sacred cavern in the Mountains of Thunder. The people call it by that name and avoid it. They have surrounded it with mystery, unholy and diabolical. In it are said to be the great treasures of the last dynasty. So terrible is the fear of the people and so great is their dread of this cavern that none will go near it. Awful tales are told of dragons that guard, sleepless and relentless, its treasure of gold and jade, of pearls and priceless rubies until the old Empire is restored. Because of this terror, no doubt, the fugitives sought refuge there.

BISHOP: It is well. It is well! The guards the entrance?

1st PRIEST: Four Brothers who watch its exit night and day.

BISHOP: How at last the Eye of God looks down upon us! This opportunity allowed by Him must not be neglected. You shall spare no efforts nor fail to use any means to capture them when you receive my orders.

[*Exit first Priest; Enter second Priest.*]

2nd PRIEST: The Viceroy's card. He is at the outer gate and wishes to know if there is any word yet of the fugitives.

BISHOP: Let him be shown here at once.

[*Exit Priest. Enter Tai Lin, who sinks in a chair beside the table and buries his head in his arms.*]

  BISHOP: Your Excellency does me great honor to pay me this visit.

  VICEROY: I cannot find her! I cannot find her!

  BISHOP: It is very unfortunate! Human frailty, alas, human frailty. It has broken my heart to find out that by being tempted he has lost his heaven. You complain bitterly. You have lost a wife; God a soul. Did you ever think that ---- that ---- perhaps the Priest was not all to blame?

  VICEROY: Yes, you are tight. She was not to blame . . . . She could do no wrong. Once I gave her a little stool. She always sat on that at my feet. You do not know, but that is the way it was. She patted my hand . . . now she is gone . . . all is gone.

  BISHOP: Did you ever see this ring? I noticed that he had this ring from your wife the first day he returned from her.   She made him promise not to part with it.   I thought it might show a little ---- a very sudden ---- I may be wrong ---- but a woman's passion.

  VICEROY: My ring?

  BISHOP: Have you ever noticed any eagerness on her part toward his coming? I did not know ---- but I suspected it. I noticed that when he was prevented from going to your palace she would send long letters to him ---- as Bishop I read them. They were filled with tender endearments, the most passionate words. It is difficult for me to speak of this, but to seek the truth has been the master work of my life. Alas, how hard it is to discover truth! To do this, one must pray to God. Since this terrible affair, I have been continually on my knees. God has smiled. His smile has penetrated the darkness surrounding this mystery and now all is clear, but to understand one has first to understand women.

  VICEROY: My wife! My wife!

  BISHOP: Woman is not a riddle; she is not an angel; she is not an enigma. She is an animal, that is all. To understand a woman, study a feline. She has all their attributes. Like them she only ceases to want when satiated. When she desires, she does nothing else . . . like an animal she follows the scent of her wishes. A woman never rests except when asleep; she never sleeps unless her hungers have been satiated. Nothing is more alarming than a woman with one eye open; like animals, when she dozes, she thinks of tomorrow's hunt. Women, as felines, have only two hungers, when these are allayed, they are at peace; when not, they prowl, they cannot help it. Hunger and reason are always in conflict, but when reason is lacking there is no contention, no delay, and they hasten on the warm trail of their desires. There are no difficulties that they will not surmount. Feline-like, they are velvety heeled. One never suspects that they have claws until they lacerate. They are not satisfied with one victim; they drain the heart's blood and sniff for another. Old age has not much blood ---- no, not very much.

  VICEROY: Tell me, where is my wife? She was like a bird and now she is gone! If you only knew her laughter, her song. What has she done?

  BISHOP: I do not know how she could have managed it. Surely she was not so bold and immodest as to come from behind the screen.

  VICEROY: From behind the screen?

  BISHOP: Yet there are worse things than that, if it had only stopped there, for the pride of beauty may have moved her unconsciously; impelled by nature she may have crept unseen to his side. This manner of movement is peculiar to women ---- and ---- snakes.

  VICEROY: She was like a little bird!

  BISHOP: Did Your Excellency know that during the first month of the world's birth these two met ---- a snake and a woman? Being unable to swallow each other, they made a perpetual compact ---- to devour man. They are alike. Their tongues have the same forked rapidity; poison lurks in their kisses; death in their embraces. One half of them is allurement; the other half desire. In gorgeous bedeckment they resemble flowers; men often mistake them for such. Their backs are beautiful with radiant color; their bellies pallid. One coaxes what the other devours. Nothing can equal the subtlety of their movement. One never feels them until they are bitten; one never knows them until the heart is clogged with their poison. Thinking them an innocent flower on account of their hues and beauty one reaches out after them and finds ---- what Your Excellency has discovered.

  VICEROY: I do not know why she did this . . . . Yes, it is all over. I am glad you have told me. She shall suffer. When you said they were animals you told the truth. I always believed that, but thought her different. I was not mistaken. She has been more snake than beast. Your words have been learned, only there is no such poison in a snake's mouth as in a woman's heart.

    BISHOP: Oh, that I could have stopped it!

    VICEROY: No, I do not ask you why you did not stop this crime when you saw its beginning, because I know you have made roguery holy to escape its responsibility and enjoy its profit. You have your own protection, but she shall die.

    BISHOP: You would have her put, to death?

    VICEROY: She shall be lingcheed ---- stripped naked before the multitude and cut into a thousand pieces.

    BISHOP: But she may be a Christian.

    VICEROY: Naked, she shall be crucified.

    BISHOP: She may be a Christian.

    VICEROY: Yes, that is her punishment by the laws of China.

    BISHOP: But she may have become a Christian.

    VICEROY: Yes, it is necessary that she shall die.

    BISHOP: She is undoubtedly a Christian by this time.

    VICEROY: What do I care if she is a Christian?

    BISHOP: Well ---- you know Christians are entitled to our protection. Yes, yes, we could not permit you to put her to death.

    VICEROY: She is my wife and by the laws of China shall be punished.

    BISHOP: Christians are not subject to your laws. They are under the protection of the church. The church does not recognize your pagan marriage. By becoming a Christian she is free and entitled to our protection.

    VICEROY: I will hammer this mission into the dust.

    BISHOP: There are three warships in the river.

VICEROY: I will sink them.

BISHOP: There are battleships at Hong Kong and ten thousand troops at Saigon. A word from me and this city shall be destroyed. Beware! Beware! Yet, I am sorry for Your Excellency.

VICEROY: You?

BISHOP: Yes, you are a wronged man. When one is cast out by a father, one can forget; when one is scorned by a son, one can grieve and forgive, but when a man's wife discards him, he cannot forget nor grieve nor forgive. Your hatred is just.

VICEROY: You?

BISHOP: Would you have me aid you?

VICEROY: You called her Christian.

BISHOP: Yes, yes, but you don't understand. You are going to act against the church, not with it. Now if you and I could come to some agreement.

VICEROY: You?

BISHOP: Yes, whereby the church agrees to withdraw its protection,

VICEROY: I agree. Where is she ---- where is she?

BISHOP: What will you agree to?

VICEROY: Anything ---- anything!

BISHOP: Will Your Excellency agree to deed your palace and its parks to the church if it withdraws its protection and sanctions her punishment.

VICEROY: No.

BISHOP: But if she is found and given over to you.

VICEROY: No. You will take my palace and lands and then squeal Christian! Christian! Christian!

BISHOP: We will draw up a contingent bond, signed and attested to the effect that the palace and lands shall not become the property of the church until she has been crucified naked before the multitude and cut into a thousand pieces.

VICEROY: The priest ---- what of him ---- the priest? (*Bishop whispers in his ear*) Make the bond. (*Turns to leave, hesitates*) You have found her?

BISHOP: Yes.

[*Viceroy totters back.*]

Curtain

Act III
Scene II

The Grotto of the Sleepless Dragon

[*Surrounding walls are composed of white glistening stalagmites and stalactites and various forms caused by calcareous excretions like snow; wood fire in center of stage; servant busy at the fire preparing the meal. The Breton, peering into the fire with a smile on his face. Seated on a high rocky bench the Wife is listening smiling and happy, to the Breton who is telling her of his native land.*]

Act III
Scene II

[*In the Grotto of the Sleepless Dragon. The Breton and the Wife seated together by the fire, the Amah busy in the background.*]

BRETON: Yes, but beautiful not alone in its wooded hills, its terraced vineyards, nor in its castles or fields or orchards; it is in its peace. The mornings there are like your laughter, the evenings like your song.

WIFE: Sunshine?

BRETON: It is far away. It seems as though it is as far distant as ---- as ----

WIFE: As what?

BRETON: As this happiness is from the pain of those past months.

WIFE: Will you never forget? Won't you forget?

BRETON: I think of them only when ----

WIFE: When you think of your native land?

BRETON: No; only when I try to understand my happiness. God but allows us to weigh our pain in the scales of joy and to ascertain our happiness by the measurement of pain. So when I think of the present the recollections of the past make me realize the true great measure of my happiness; while the thought of our joys in that land where all is peace is only intensified by the remembrance of the pain that we shall never again feel.

WIFE: Oh, if we were only where the sun shines! . . . . Tell me again ---- the flowers, the sky, the sun. When will we see the sun again?

BRETON: The sun will shine every day in the land where we will live. Our home is on a hill and on all sides are farmsteads in their closures with the blue smoke climbing slowly from their chimneys as though reluctant to leave them. Pigeons cover the barn roofs and chickens ----

WIFE: (*Laughing gaily*) Chickens! You have chickens? Oh, how I love to hear the little ones go cheep! cheep! cheep! I shall have hundreds of them and will feed them with my own hands. I will find their nests. They cannot hide them from me. Oh, tell me, tell me, when will we go?

BRETON: I don't know.

WIFE: You don't know? You don't ----

BRETON: Yes, yes, we will go soon.

WIFE: Then let us go now! This is a tomb. It is the tomb of my race, and who knows ----

BRETON: There is no danger, no one know ----

WIFE: But the dream! Tell him the dream, Amah.

BRETON: Do not tremble. You must not. Dreams are nothing but the mist clouds of day that memories blow across the darkened dome of night.

WIFE: Yes, I know that you will call this dream just some airy tapestry of sleep; strangely woven, perhaps, but still the gauzy slumber work of my foolish mind. Yet, yet . . . .

BRETON: Do not cry. It is nothing.

WIFE: (*Sobbing*) It was the spider ---- the crimson spider ----

AMAH: Do not cry, my lady, do no cry! Dreams are only reflections in the great river. How can these reflections stem the river or alter the course of our craft?

BRETON: Do not cry. We will go away.

WIFE: We will go ---- out in the sunshine?

BRETON: Yes, tomorrow.

WIFE: (*Rising with laughter*) Amah! Amah! We are going away ---- out into the sunshine! And tomorrow, Amah, we are going to leave tomorrow! Come we must hurry dinner (*assists the Amah*) and then pack. What happiness it is to pack. And think of it when next we unpack it will be in that land where there is only sunshine and where dawn is like laughter and evening like a song.

AMAH: Listen! I hear a noise!

WIFE: (*Laughing*) A noise! Oh, it is only an echo in the great thoroughfare of life. And, how, Amah, can echoes stop the passers-on or alter our course?

AMAH: It may be, but ----

WIFE: We must hurry, Amah, so we can pack. Nothing has so much of happiness. To pack is to anticipate, and oh, with what happy thought will the laying away of each garment fill our minds. For we are going a long way ---- beyond the Five Seas. Then we will unpack ---- and that will be to remember, which is next best the foretasting of our expectations. In our trunks are our lives;

in their packing and unpacking the changes that mark the rise and fall of our hopes. Tragedies as well as trousseaux are packed in them. So come, Amah, we must hurry.

    AMAH: Yes, my lady we must hurry! But that dream.

    WIFE: (*Laughing*) That dream? Why, what childishness is this, Amah? Do you not know that dreams are but the contorted images of our fears such as the lanterns of night cast upon the darkness to frighten timid souls? You are robbed, yet you lose nothing; you are killed, yet you do not die; you become rich or poor; old or young and yet you wake as you went to sleep.

    AMAH: I know, my lady, but what follows? When the mistress commands the servant obeys; when one weeps, it means sorrow; when the cook crows, it is dawn; lightning portends a storm; a frown anger; a dagger death ---- but dreams, my lady, what do dreams . . . .

    WIFE: Ah, Amah, what does it mean? Don't let us talk of it; we are going away tomorrow . . . . Isn't dinner ready now? (*To the Breton*) To what are you listening?

    BRETON: It must be the sound of the waterfall.

    WIFE: You hear something?

    BRETON: Listen!

    WIFE: Is it very long until tomorrow?

    BRETON: No, for we will leave here at dawn.

    WIFE: We are going away at dawn, Amah; we will see the dawn and then the sunrise. (*Laughing*) The sun! The sun! In a few hours we will be like birds free out in the sunlight! Now I am as happy as when I broke the bars of the cage that man made and gilded for me. At dawn, Amah, at dawn!

    AMAH: That dream . . . .

    WIFE: (*Laying her hands on the shoulders of the Breton*) It will not be long, will it?

    BRETON: (*Endeavors to take her in his arms but she breaks laughing from him*) Why do you torture me?

WIFE: Torture me?

BRETON: Do you not know that it is possible to rack the heart more violently with tempted joys or those delayed than by pain? So now you force me so long the silent keeper of my pain, to become the oppressor of my love and the goaler of my happiness.

WIFE: (*With mocking laughter*) You? How can you be the oppressor of love? You a feeble man and love the despot of every human heart! You the gaoler of your happiness! Why that is to encompass another world and be monarch of it from horizon to horizon and in that world of happiness we go as guests and not as conquerors; we are invited and dismissed; we go into and out of that world as it sees fit. You the gaoler of it!

BRETON: If you but knew ----

WIFE: I don't I know? Is not this darkness as hourless and endless to me as to you? But at dawn are we not going away? Then, when we are in your country where is peace, you may ----

AMAH: Listen!

WIFE: (*Placing her hands on his shoulders*) Do not look that way! To see so much sadness in this gloom frightens me. (*Laughing softly*) If you will promise me not to ---- you know ---- I will ---- Just once ----

[*Breton puts his arms about her.*]

AMAH: Listen!

[*A distant noise is heard which gradually becomes more distinct. The Breton puts the Wife aside and goes out. The noise approaches and the rumble of voices is heard. Breton re-enters, pallid and with slow footsteps. Lays his hand gently on the shoulder of the Wife.*]

BRETON: They have found us.

WIFE: No, no! We are going away at dawn!

BRETON: Yes, they have found us. The priests are coming.

WIFE: We are going away at dawn, Amah (*Sinks fainting to the floor*)

BRETON: (*On his knees beside her*) Speak! Speak to me! I will take you away. No one shall find you ....

Enter priests with flaring torches and surrounds them.

1st PRIEST: (*Touching Breton on the shoulder*) Come!

Curtain

Act IV
Scene I

Time -- Early Morning

The Ancestral Hall of Tai Lin's Palace

[*The rear of the stage shows the altar upon which are placed the ancestral tablets of Tai Lin's father's, before which are burning bowls of oil, papers and incense. Front of the altar are three ebony chairs and three tables.*

In the right hand chair is Tai Lin seated, his head buried in his arms. To the left enters the Bishop accompanied by French Consul Commandant and a number of priests. Takes seat in the center chair. Magistrate enters accompanied by various officials and clerks. Takes chair on the left. Bishop's retinue is seated to the left and Magistrate's retinue to the right.

To the right is an oval doorway hung with a curtain, through which the Wife eaters.]

Act IV
Scene I

[*Ancestral hall of Tai Lin. The Judgment. The Viceroy is seated in one of the three chairs placed before the ancestral tablets. Presently the Bishop and French Consul with their retinues enter. Bishop occupies the center chair while the others take seats along the right side of the hall. Enter Chinese Magistrate with his retinue. He occupies the chair next to the Bishop while his retinue is ranged along the left aide of the hall.*]

MAGIST: (*Raising his hand*) Let the prisoner be brought in.

[*A curtain is drawn from an oval aperture on the right wall showing the Wife standing in a shaft of morning sunlight. She steps lightly in, then presses back against the doorway.*]

Come forward before this court (*Wife only presses more closely against the curtains*).

BISHOP: (*To Magistrate*) Do not frighten her, but let the charges be read.

[*Magistrate raises his hand and the First Clerk on the left rises.*]

1st CLERK: Tai Luk Man, on the night of the Propitiation of the Gods of the Waters you stole away with or were stolen by a French priest living in the Catholic mission of Yangching, and for more than one moon you lived alone with him in the Grotto of the Sleeping Dragon. By this deed you violated or were forced to violate, those laws of the Empire which, by the wisdom of the Great Ancients, were made to conserve the domestic relations of the people of the Middle Kingdom. And so shall you or he be punished according to your deserts, or shall, because of your merits, be commended for mercy to the great emperor.

MAGIST: Let the witnesses testify.

[*Bishop raises his hand.*]

1st PRIEST: On the 20th day of this, moon, by the command, of his Lordship the Bishop, myself with eleven other priests went to the Grotto of the Sleepless Dragon and there in one of its darkened chambers we came upon this woman and a former priest of our Mission. We seized them and brought them hither, and gave them into the possession of his Lordship the Bishop.

2nd PRIEST: When we entered the cavern in which they were concealed it was in darkness. There we found her lying upon the floor with her head resting upon his bosom.

BISHOP: You saw what?

2nd PRIEST: We saw her lying upon the floor with her head resting upon his bosom.

BISHOP: That will do.

3rd PRIEST: By the lights of our torches, we discovered them in the uttermost recesses of the cavern. It was only with difficulty that we discovered them. Finally when we did find them by the aid of their torches, we found this woman lying in the arms of our former brother.

VICEROY: (*With a choking cry*) Kill!

WIFE: (*Going swiftly over to the Viceroy falls upon her knees before the table and looks up into his face*) My husband, do not do that! You do not know how it hurt. No, no, you must not ---- I have done wrong. Do not be angry and cry out as you did. It was terrible for you to do that because it is all over and I have suffered more than all these yamen-men can lay upon me. Forgive me, my husband; send these men away. You do not know how they frighten me. Won't you forgive me? You must not let these two moons of fault outweigh my years of love. Don't you remember how I used to sit on a stool at your feet? and you let me pull your ears? Won't you forgive me, my husband?

VICEROY: Where is he?

WIFE: No, no, you must not. He just came each day and went away. I do not know how it happened. At first I did not understand. Then I tried to harden my heart, but each day when he returned my frozen resolution melted as the sun of the fourth moon melts the earth's bosom and brings forth again the verdure of spring . . . . As a swimmer in the sea was my little heart in the deep blue of his eyes. Each day their tides overwhelmed my strength and bore me away on their flood.

VICEROY: (*Choking*) Where is he?

WIFE: No, no, he did no wrong ---- his love was not other than the will-less tide that the sunlight from heaven ----

[*Tai Lin brings his fist down on the table and the Wife falls sobbing to the floor.*]

BISHOP: (*To Magistrate*) Question her.

MAGIST: Do you confess your guilt? (*No answer but her sobs*) Did you not live with this priest in the Sleepless Dragon Cavern?

[*Wife again lifts her hands to Tai Lin.*]

BISHOP: This is very sad, but it is necessary that justice be done. This Wife insists that she is innocent . . . . some one must be guilty. If she is without sin our former brother must have stolen her away and upon him punishment must fall. If she is innocent, he must be guilty and so must die. Yes, he must die. (*Wife's sobs cease. She looks dumbly into the Bishop's face*) The guilty alone must suffer punishment and die.

WIFE: No, no!

BISHOP: We must have Justice for the knowledge of our uprightness is spread over all countries and the people look for us for it.

WIFE: (*Holding out her hands to him*) Oh, why do you say that? Is it not better to give mercy than demand justice? I know you men of greatness love justice, but it is so deep, while mercy is like the heavens where every little act shines out as the light of a star and tinges the depths of whole regions. Oh, Great Sir, do not be just and your fame will spread over all lands; nothing is so wide as mercy. Wherever the skies cast their shadow, wherever stars shine, wherever dews fall from heaven, man will love you. Oh, do not hurt him ---- if you only knew ----

[*Tai Lin brings his fist down on the table.*]

BISHOP: If he is guilty, he must die.

WIFE: (*Rising presently to her feet*) I am guilty.

MAGIST: What! do you confess?

WIFE: Yes.

MAGIST: You confess to all charges?

WIFE: Yes.

BISHOP: Did you persuade the brother of our mission to flee with you?

WIFE: Yes.

[*Tai Lin rises, overturning the table before him, passes half down the hall, suddenly stops, clutches at his throat, falls, and is carried from the hall.*]

  MAGIST: Does he mean that?

  BISHOP: Yes.

  MAGIST: Let the priest be brought in that he may witness her death warrant. (*Breton is brought in bound and gagged to rear of hall by soldiers*) She shall be given the silken scarf, that she may die in the seclusion of her own chamber.

  BISHOP: What! Is that according to his complaint? Would you dare defraud the law?

  MAGIST: You would not ---- you would not insist that she die on the crucifix . . . .

  BISHOP: Yes, that is the law, and the law must be executed.

  MAGIST: I cannot do it! I cannot do it!

  BISHOP: It is his demand. It is the law of the empire. Dare you fail to enforce it?

  MAGIST: Bring me the Vermilion Pencil. (*Signs the warrant*) It is done.

  BISHOP: Remember that I hold you responsible for the execution of this woman according to the law, on the river bank at sunset. Beware that she does not die before then.

[*Magistrate leaves the room followed by his retinue with the exception of the First Clerk. Bishop leans back in his chair. One of the priests speaks to him; he rises hastily and as he passes the Wife looks up. Bishop whispers to her and she clasps her hands together uttering a joyous cry. Exit Bishop and priests.*]

  1st CLERK: (*Brusquely*) Foolish woman, why did you confess?

  WIFE: (*Lightly*) Oh, I did not know what else to do.

  1st CLERK: (*Gruffly*) No doubt, but it is not the first time a woman's tongue has been the knife to lingchee her body.

  WIFE: (*Mockingly*) Indeed!

1st CLERK: (*Harshly*) Woman, why did you lie? (*She turns away*) Why did you lie?

WIFE: (*With gay raillery*) Oh, I don't know. Don't you see I but follow the ways of nature wherein the straightest tree is felled the soonest and the cleanest well is first drunk up; wherein the most innocent bird is quickest netted and the tenderest flower is first plucked that it, for one fleeting moment, might pleasure man's nostril? Thus, in such fashion, Mr. Clerk, must my uprightness be out down; my good name and virtue drunk up; my innocence destroyed and coffined while the little flower of my life is plucked and cast aside .... Oh, well, I do not grieve. The silken scarf is for the neck. Whoever heard of it strangling the heart?

1st CLERK: Unfortunate woman! There is to be no silken scarf for you.

WIFE: What do you mean?

1st CLERK: Woman, do you not know the law? You are to die naked before the multitude.

[*Breton struggles ineffectually with soldiers at end of hall.*]

WIFE: No! No! (*She sways and falls down at the feet of the 1st Clerk, clutching his robes*) No! No! They have all gone and left me but you. Won't you save me? No! No! You must not go! (*She clings to his robe as he moves along*) Talk with me! How can you leave? Listen! Why can I not have in all this wide house of the world just one little corner to die in?

1st CLERK: I can do nothing. You die at sunset by the lingchee.

[*Wife rises, sways, looks wildly round the room, sees Breton at end of the hall ---- starts toward him with outstretched hands ---- swoons.*]

Curtain

Act IV
Scene II

[*Time: Just before sunset.

The Bund: In the rear center is seen a crucifix, two black stones and a tub. To the left rear is a dais under red canopy on which are three chairs. Scene opens on patrol of French marines and a small picket of Chinese soldiers. Many people begin to arrive, in various costumes. Enter by ladder from rear of stage from Bund after salute has been fired, Bishop followed by French officers and priests ---- crowd on Bund bows respectfully ---- soldiers and marines present arms. Bishop moves haughtily to chairs under canopy and with slight hesitation occupies center chair.

Kettledrums, etc. announce approach of Magistrate, preceded by three executioners who take their place beside crucifix. Magistrate occupies seat to left of the Bishop and before him is placed a table with a crimson cloth and the vermilion pencil. Silently a solitary sedan enters and is carried over to the dais and Tai Lin haggard and feeble totters out of it. Apparently oblivious to surroundings sinks into chair at Bishop's right.

Enter sedan in blue and white. Wife steps daintily out and seeing Bishop moves with a smile toward him. He draws away from her in horror. At this she perceives her husband, falls on her knees and clasps his legs in her arms. Presently he reaches out his hand and strokes her on the head. At signal from the Magistrate two executioners step forward and drag her over to the crucifix and bind her. As one tears off her silken jacket Tai Lin rises to his feet; tries to speak but cannot; totters and sinks to the ground dead.

Wife is unbound and revised. Again at a signal from Magistrate is seized by the executioners and bound to the crucifix. As her other garments are about to be torn from her, after one arm and shoulder have been laid bare there is heard in the distance a great noise. This draws nearer; finally there is distinguished the battlecry of the Deluge Family. Consternation and crowd rushes hither and thither. Soon a great multitude swarms on the stage ---- they make way and the Breton enters clothed in black with the Symbol gleaming on his breast. He stands a moment gazing before him; draws his hands across his eyes and shakes his head and shoulders as if to waken himself from stupor. Advances toward crucifix; executioners fall on their knees and strike their heads on the ground twice.

Breton picks up one of the executioner's swords and severs thongs that bind the Wife. Clasping her to him he draws his robe around her and slowly steps back to the edge of the Bund. Darkness falls with them standing on the edge of the Bund and the crowd silent abound them.]

Act IV
Scene II

[Sunset at the execution grounds on the river bank. Three chairs to the left on a raised dais under a red canopy. In front of chairs is a crucifix and small tub. In the background

the river with the French gunboats and Chinese junks; beyond the dragon roofs and pagodas of Honan, beyond these the purple tops of distant mountains. The assembled multitude stands in the form of a crescent about the crucifix; petty mandarins in official gold-brocaded robes; Manchus in silken robes, red coated soldiers, French marines in blue and white uniforms. Over all silence.]

    1st MANDARIN: Strange things will happen today.

    2nd MANDARIN: Will you look when she is tied upon that crucifix?

    1st MANDARIN: Strange things will happen today.

    2nd MANDARIN: Naked ---- by the code ---- naked.

    1st MANDARIN: Listen!

    2nd MANDARIN: Listen?

    1st MANDARIN: Did you hear a cry?

    2nd MANDARIN: A cry? A woman's cry?

    1st MANDARIN: No, multitudes! Armies!

[Enter Bishop followed by French officers, seats himself in center chair on dais.]

    1st MANDARIN: How white he is.

    2nd MANDARIN: How cold!

    1st MANDARIN: He shall see strange things today.

    3rd MANDARIN: They say that the abyss of Tai Lung vomits forth black vapors.

    1st MANDARIN: Listen!

[Kettledrums are heard. The Magistrate enters in sedan chair, preceded by the executioners and takes chair to left of Bishop.]

    3rd MANDARIN: This is one day I would not be the Magistrate.

    2nd MANDARIN: He will see her ---- her ----

1st MANDARIN: He? He shall see strange things ---- terrible things.

2nd MANDARIN: Terrible things?

1st MANDARIN: Yes, terror is abroad today.

3rd MANDARIN: You mean?

2nd MANDARIN: Tai Lin is coming.

[*Tai Lin enters in sedan unattended and seats himself to right of Bishop.*]

3rd MANDARIN: Is he alive?

2nd MANDARIN: I doubt it.

3rd MANDARIN: Look at his eyes.

1st MANDARIN: What terror shall they look upon this day ---- what dreadful terror.

[*Enter sedan of the Wife; she steps out and going before Tai Lin she holds out her hands to him, then falling before him clasps his legs in her arms.*]

BISHOP: (*To Magistrate with an imperious gesture toward the Wife*) Let the law be done.

[*Magistrate raises the vermilion pencil and the executioners drag the Wife to the crucifix. Enter Fourth Mandarin.*]

4th MANDARIN: Have you heard? The Deluge has risen!

2nd & 3rd MANDARIN: No, no.

1st MANDARIN: Yes, terrible things will happen tonight.

4th MANDARIN: The priest has escaped from his prison and with the Great Symbol of the Deluge on his bosom like an eye from hell, he is coming here followed by ten times ten thousand men. Flee! Flee!

[*Exit 4th Mandarin*]

2nd MANDARIN: Look! Look!

[*Executioners tear off Wife's outer garments and tie her to the crucifix. Executioner starts to tear off her jacket. Tai Lin rises then falls back lifeless in his chair. Consternation sweeps over the multitude.*]

MAGIST: The Great Man, Tai Lin, is dead. He alone was the accuser. The prisoner is free.

[*Executioners cut her free from crucifix. She lies limp at foot of the crucifix.*]

BISHOP: (*Rising and lifting his hand imperiously*) How is it that a Magistrate of the Middle Kingdom dares hush up a public crime? This guilty woman was taken in the midst of her sin. In her trial she confessed her guilt and was condemned by the law and her husband's demand. Dare a Magistrate do contrary to this? Let him beware!

MAGIST: Does the eldest son of the Great Man Tai demand death? . . . . (*No answer*) . . . . Does any member of the Tai family demand death? . . . . (*No reply*) . . . . Does any man of the Middle Kingdom demand the cutting into pieces of this woman? . . . . reply. (*To the Bishop triumphantly*) She is free!

BISHOP: Ah!

MAGIST: It is in accordance with the law.

BISHOP: Ah?

MAGIST: No one demands it.

BISHOP: Ah?

MAGIST: You have no legal right.

BISHOP: (*Drawing paper from his robe and throwing it on the table*) There is my legal right.

[*Magistrate reads paper and presently lifts again the vermilion pencil and the unconscious Wife is again bound upon the crucifix. The executioners cut away the left shoulder of her robe. The first stroke is about to be given.*]

A multitude in the distance: Hung Shun Tien! Hung Shun Tien!

[*Consternation in the multitude on the Bund. Enter Breton followed by the Deluge. He approaches the crucifix.*]

      BRETON: (*Softly*) I have come! (*Wife smiles faintly*) I have come! (*Wife's laughter*)

[*Breton cuts the cords from the Wife; draws his black robe about her while her head nestles beside the Great Symbol on his bosom. Breton carrying the Wife in left arm and the executioner's sword in his right moves to the river's edge. Wife reaches up and draws his head down to hers. Night falls.*]

Curtain

Made in the USA
Columbia, SC
05 December 2024